A SWEETNESS

RISING

D1525736

A   S W E E T N E S S

RISING

New and Selected Poems

R O B E R T A   S P E A R

Edited with an Introduction

B Y   P H I L I P   L E V I N E

G R E A T   V A L L E Y   B O O K S
H E Y D A Y   B O O K S, Berkeley, California

For Sophia and Eli

Some of the poems in *A Sweetness Rising* first appeared in *The Great River Review, Raritan, Crazy Horse, The Alaska Poetry Review, The San Joaquin Review, Runes, Poetry, Vision, The Geography of Home, Highway 99,* and *How Much Earth: The Fresno Poets.*

Silks (Holt, Rinehart and Winston, 1980) included poems first published in *The New Yorker, Quarterly West, Valley Light, Missouri Review,* and *Seneca Review.*

Taking to Water (Holt, Rinehart and Winston, 1984) included poems first published in *The New Yorker, Memphis Review, Poetry,* and *American Poetry Review.*

The Pilgrim Among Us (Wesleyan University Press, 1991) included poems first published in *Field, Missouri Review, Memphis Review, Poetry, Ploughshares, Raccoon,* and *Redstart.* Reprinted by permission of Wesleyan University Press.

The author wanted to thank the National Endowment for the Humanities for a grant that aided in the completion of this book. Also, a special thanks to Jean, Peter, and Phil for their help along the way.

Philip Levine thanks Sandra Hoben and Peter Everwine for their advice and all their help in making this collection possible.

Library of Congress Cataloging-in-Publication Data

Spear, Roberta.
     A sweetness rising : new and selected poems / Roberta Spear ; edited and with an introduction by Philip Levine.
          p. cm.
     ISBN 978-1-59714-063-8 (pbk. : alk. paper)
     1. Central Valley (Calif. : Valley)—Poetry. I. Title.
     PS3569.P395S94 2007
     811'.54—dc22
                                        2007003257

Cover Photo: *Sesimbra* by Micha Langer, 1995. Courtesy of the photographer.
Cover Design: Lorraine Rath
Interior Design/Typesetting: Leigh McLellan Design
Printing and Binding: McNaughton & Gunn, Saline, MI

Orders, inquiries, and correspondence should be addressed to:
     Heyday Books
     P. O. Box 9145, Berkeley, CA 94709
     (510) 549-3564, Fax (510) 549-1889
     www.heydaybooks.com

Printed in the United States of America

10 9 8 7 6 5 4 3 2 1

CONTENTS

FROM *THE PILGRIM AMONG US* (1991)

INTRODUCTION

In the Next World: The Poetry of Roberta Spear

WHEN ROBERTA SPEAR died of leukemia in the spring of 2003, she left behind not only a grieving family, but also an almost completed fourth book of poems. Thirty years earlier, when her husband was assigned to a hospital in Fresno to do his residency, she'd returned from Winston-Salem, North Carolina, where he had studied medicine and she had taught creative writing. Thus she was back in the Central Valley where she'd grown up in the town of Hanford, some thirty miles south of Fresno. Now she was not only a poet but also the mother of a son and soon a daughter. For as long as she lived she gave herself totally to the roles of wife, mother, poet, and friend to the cluster of poets settled in and around Fresno. California's Central Valley is one of the keys to her poetry, for above all else Roberta was a poet of "person, place, and thing." The people of central California are the people of more than half her poems; the landscape and the climate of scorching summers and fog-bound winters appear and disappear in these poems. The Valley, as it's known here, is not the California of the movies, unless the movie you have in mind is *The Grapes of Wrath,* for it is exactly the place to which the Joads arrive on their trek from Oklahoma with all their hopes for a better life soon to go unfulfilled. In Hanford she would have grown up with the children of the Joads or people like them who shared that journey, as well as the children of farmers and ranchers and the Chicanos and African Americans who worked in their fields, orchards, and vineyards. And she would have watched with them as the years brought smog, chronic unemployment, and gang warfare. Once it may have been the rural idyll described by John Muir when he first crossed the Pacheco Pass and beheld it from the north. Now it is Twenty-First-Century America, the small towns bursting with the new immigrants from Southeast Asia and the American rust belt.

How could a poet find so much to sing about in a place like this, for sing is what she did? From her poem "Two Trees":

And from the kitchen table,
I can see the shadows shift
as the pecan breathes in the sunlight.
I wonder if this giant,
the grandfather of our back field,
still has what it takes
under these tendons of bark,
the layers riddled by seasons of birds,
or if the young dogwood tipped with green
will surprise us next March.

There are two crucial words in that passage: wonder and surprise. By some amazing alchemy Spear seemed able to waken each day—or at least each day that's recorded in her poetry—with a sense of wonder in the presence of the physical world as though each dawn were a surprise, an event like none other in the history of experience. There is a kind of primal innocence in her poetry; she sees a world untainted by the brutal forces that have turned the Valley into an ongoing catastrophe. It's not that she was unaware or ignorant of what was around her; it's simply that the present with all its riches, with all the majesty of its being tangible, was amazing to her, a gift, each moment a moment of miraculous potential, and she saw her function as a poet to observe it, to detail it, to name it, and when all her forces as an artist were at her command, to bless it. And those forces were hers more often than not. The answer to the question that began this paragraph—how could she sing?—is mysterious and has much to do with her sense of fulfillment as a woman as well as the glory of her individual being.

She was always a creature of hope. In all the years I knew her, I never knew her to despair.

And I knew her for thirty-four years, since she was a very young woman enrolled in an advanced class in poetry writing at Fresno State, a class that someone had let swell to forty students. That first evening the class met in a cavernous, unadorned chemistry lab that appalled me, I behaved very badly on purpose, for I was determined to get it down to something manageable and to move the smaller class to a more intimate setting, and to do so I set about terrifying the students. Each week, I told them, you'll be required to hand in a new poem in whatever form I require: for example thirty lines of anapestic tetrameter without an adjective. Perhaps twenty heroic couplets in the style of Charles Churchill, a blank verse monologue in the voice of Henry Ford on the theme of the Jews. When I paused to take a breath, a fresh young blonde woman asked if I recognized free verse. I said that I did, and that I'd seen a lot of it of late. She informed me that in Galway Kinnell's class at UC Irvine, the students decided what forms they wrote in. I mused for a moment and replied that it was an interesting notion. Kinnell was certainly a marvelous poet, who—I noted—had written brilliantly in traditional forms early in his writing life. It worked: the next week only sixteen students showed up, the others had dropped. And the blonde? She was of course Roberta Spear. Kinnell had advised her to come to Fresno if she were serious about becoming a poet, and she was not about to be discouraged by my folderol. As the weeks passed I began to discover her poems and also to discover the iron-willed person who had written them.

A few years later she enrolled in a translation class I taught with the Spanish critic and scholar José Elgorriaga, and I believe it was there that she discovered the poetry of Rafael Alberti, Gloria Fuertes, and Pablo Neruda. She loved the sharp tongue and quick wit of Fuertes' poems, that talking back men of prestige and power and the whole rigged system that was Franco's Spain in which an ordinary working woman might drown without anyone noticing. But for her Neruda was supreme—a poet the likes of whom she had never before encountered—for it was in his work, her friend Sandra Hoben writes, she found "the difference between most poetry and what the greats were up to." His *Odas Elementales* were especially significant, for it was in them that the great Chilean honors the things of everyday—a suit, a pinch of salt, an onion, a pair of socks, the color green—so as to create an event of cosmic significance, and he does it with wit, style, at times an almost preposterous vocabulary, and always with a smile. After Neruda her aims in poetry were never the same; she now had a standard, a far clearer notion of "the poem" she was after.

At a time when so many young women poets were discovering and bathing in the river that was Plath, Spear was almost totally uninterested: she wrote that she resented "the common association between the woman poet, neurosis, and kitchen sinks." In fact she was far more interested in the poetry of Ted Hughes with its extraordinary evocations of beasts and men and the pure energy that drives his lyrics forward toward an apocalyptic moment. Not that she ever tried to imitate his raucous, grinding music nor ever accepted his vision of the eternal war among all creatures; the music of her poetry is far quieter and more adapted to her own vision in which the individual often merges with the *other*. In terms of the music of her poetry, D. H. Lawrence, especially in his superb Rhine Valley poems, was truly influential. Her poetry arrived, she wrote, "especially when [she was] overwhelmed by the pure physicalness of myself, other people, or my surroundings." In a singular way she envisioned herself as another aspect of her environment, the one gifted with the language to speak for all the individual creations that made up her world. That Nerudaesque urge to blend with all things and to give all things their voice you can hear swelling in many of her finest poems.

> Yet, a few things can be explained
> by all this racket. Life must be named,
> called back often before it wanders too far.
> And so, a mother lifts her skirt
> and slowly wades into the water

after a child who would rather follow
the fish to their smoky depths.
Also, there are always those
who mean nothing when they speak,
who, like birds, love the sound of air so much
they wave their arms, their tongues
and give it away.
    (from "Cinque Terre: The Land of Five Noises")

One reviewer of her first book (Robert Peters in *The American Book Review*) wrote of her "quiet, hard-seeing way of moving at, into, and through natural objects, assimilating them into her vision." Another (Joseph Parisi in *The Chicago Tribune)* praised her gift for metaphor and imagery that suggest "the mysterious depths beneath her shining surfaces." In a prose statement in the anthology *What Will Suffice* she illuminates the source of her poem "Diving for Atlantis":

> At the time I wrote "Diving for Atlantis," I was pregnant with my first child and living in the South (North Carolina). The world around me seemed unbelievably vibrant and intriguing. The children who swam around me at the local "Y" demonstrated what I had already learned as a poet—that the imagination has an infinite capacity for transforming one's identity and surroundings....Just as the children dive into the water to look for the mythical city of Atlanta, the poet must penetrate the layers of the imagination until the vision is realized.

Writing of her final book, *The Pilgrim Among Us*, the poet Edward Hirsch described her as a poet who "transfigures the ordinary and pinpoints the mysteries of daily life...." And Margaret Gibson, commenting on the same book, wrote that in Spear's poetry "it's the ordinary which is discovered to be the site of the extraordinary." Anyone who reads her will be struck by her ability to focus her attention on that which often seems beneath our attention, and find there the source of her own visionary poems. One of her favorite poems was "Grappa in September" by the great Italian poet Cesare Pavese, which she read both in the Italian and in the translation of William Arrowsmith. It is not a typical Pavese poem; Pavese in the poems of *Hard Labor* is most often a narrative poet, but in this poem nothing happens. The poem is merely a description of a northern Italian village at the end of summer. We discover the house at the field's edge that sells tobacco "which is blackish in color / and tastes of sugar… / They also have grappa there, the color of water." The final stanza begins:

> This is the time when every man should stand
> still in the street and see how everything ripens.

If Spear saw this poem as a metaphor for her own work I do not know, but I do know that she read it over and over, and that she found in it an almost mystical sense of what the poetry she loved was capable of. I know also that she was much taken with a remark of Pavese's from his book on American literature: "The new symbolism of Whitman meant, not the allegorical structures of Dante but a…sort of double vision through which, from the single object of the senses vividly absorbed and possessed, there radiates a sort of halo of unexpected spirituality." It was of course that aspect of American poetry, which she found first in Whitman, Williams, and especially Stevens, and later in the contemporaries she most valued, that she worked to incorporate in her own work.

*

Rereading her poetry I cannot hear the least suggestion of a familiarity with my poetry or the poetry of her first poetry writing teacher, Galway Kinnell, but one teacher had a profound effect on the voice she created for herself or the voice that found her in her mature poems, and that was the voice of Peter Everwine. She had already studied Antonio Machado and Juan Ramón Jiménez and admired the crystalline quality and the precision that is the hallmark of their work. She caught echoes of something similar in those delicate love poems of Lawrence, but the first time she encountered it in an American voice was in Everwine's work. Here is that voice in a poem from his second book, *Keeping the Night,* "Perossa Canavese," written shortly after his first trip to the village of his ancestors:

What I came for
—all those miles—
was to see the face of the village
my people spoke of
in the hour before sleep,
and which I was given for my own
like an empty locket,
like a mirror in a locked room.

In a poem from her first book called "The Traveler," dedicated to Everwine, she answers him in that new voice that will become the voice of much of her poetry.

At the edge of the village,
battered stalks and then a field
of poppies. You drop your pack
to the ground, picking
the few that will last
until you find others.

Among the stalks,
an old farmer
whose plow has died.
Wearing these flowers
you remind him of his son
who let the fields
go to seed. Not everyone
will be quick to claim you…

This was written twenty-five years ago after her second trip to Italy, and it constitutes the first poem in an extended conversation with her former teacher.

Her first trip to Italy in 1967, and especially the second in '80, were of momentous importance in her development as a person and a poet. She literally fell in love with the people and the landscape, and they appear in many of the poems that were to follow. (She would return to Italy two more times, the last time in 2000 with her son and daughter.) She also fell in love with the language to which she devoted years of study so that she might read the poets whose language it was, from Dante to Ungaretti, Pavese and Sinisgalli. And occasionally translate them. Much as she admired Everwine's voice and his strategies, there was in Spear a natural volubility, a sense of luxury and abundance that was absent in Everwine's work. His line suited her perfectly and she retained it for the rest of her career, but his rigorous sense of economy, the total absence of the baroque in his writing, that urge that her earlier love and study of Neruda's odes had nurtured couldn't find room to expand and play unless she let go. This created a tension that the poems themselves exploited, for Roberta's poems had the habit of seeking a larger, more expansive format, and she had the good sense to let them. She also had a strong sense of narrative; she wanted to tell in verse the family stories she inherited, to become as it were the family mythmaker. Indeed she found stories everywhere, but like her beloved Pavese she found them mostly in the ordinary people who inhabited the various neighborhoods that had been or were to become home. And since home for the last three decades of her life was Fresno, they frequently became the stories of American immigrants, especially those from Asia and Mexico. You could say at times she saw stories where there were none or where she simply invented them, exotic stories of gypsies and pranksters, travelers and seekers, those with whom she identified. This is most obvious in what is for me her finest book, *Taking to Water,* which is truly a volume of magic, one that transforms the ordinary things of daily life into tales to conjure with, as in the conclusion of "Map for the Unborn":

> Follow the line that runs
> from the thumb to the heart
> until lines cover your face

and your legs give in.
Circle the mound of your smallest finger
twice around the world
until your fortune comes and goes
and a villager opens his window
to call you inside.
He will take your hand
and ask to hear your stories,
for you have crossed the seas
of your mother, and who can remember
having traveled so far?

In the last years of her life she found new works to admire, poets she hadn't known, and with her usual generosity of spirit she touted them (I'm thinking especially of the late books of Larry Levis and Ruth Stone and *New Addresses* by Kenneth Koch and *Time and Money* by William Matthews) more than she pushed her own work. The discovery of a true poet that mattered was an extraordinary event for her; Zbigniew Herbert, Milosz, Syzmborska, Sabines, Nancy Willard, she came back to again and again. On several occasions I loaded her down with the books I'd received in the mail, and her joy at what treasures they might hold was lovely to behold. In truth she never pushed her own work. She decided early on she disliked giving poetry readings, and although she knew this had become one of the chief means by which a poet built a reputation and a following, she found the expenditure of nervous energy not worth the product. Furthermore they caused a disturbance in the normal flow of her life, they took her away from the primary task, which was the making of the poems. If this meant she would publish less and sell fewer copies of those books she published, so be it. This was a decision she made before she was thirty, and she never looked back.

She also made her peace with the Valley. Most of the poets who studied with her at Fresno State—Larry Levis, David St. John, Greg Pape, Gary Soto—got out as soon as they could. Italy may have been where her heart was, but Fresno was where her husband practiced medicine, her children went to school, and she wrote her best poems. For the anthology *The Geography of Home* she wrote a prose introduction to her poems that addressed exactly that.

> Over the last thirty years, I have come to learn that two essential components of this celebratory tradition in poetry are passion and careful observation. While I was never lacking in the first, the second was a task made all the more difficult by living in a place that often seemed desolate and impoverished. Difficult, but not impossible. Even now, if you drive east a few miles into the countryside or the nearby foothills, the fields of yellow grass with their outcroppings of rock and skeletal oaks are still reminiscent in their rugged beauty of parts of southern Europe.

If she couldn't live in the Italy she loved she was determined to find a way of bringing the country of her devotion to the Valley, and she did exactly that with her poetry.

In a singular poem entitled "Geraniums" from her book *The Pilgrim Among Us* she wrote,

> In the next world, I will be the one
> forever pushing open
> the warped green shutters to let
> the sunlight enter the room…

I wouldn't be surprised if that were true, but what I know for certain is that in this world Roberta was constantly pushing aside the shutters to let light in. The young woman I encountered over thirty years ago would never let well enough pass for wisdom. She wanted to know why: why this word and not that? Why this poem or any poem at all? My initial impulse was to urge Valium on her, but as that first semester wore on I realized I had someone rare, a truth seeker who let nothing stop her. Over the years of our friendship whenever I wanted to revive my belief in the value of writing poetry or living a moral life, I would call on Roberta, either in her poetry or in her person, and she was always there for me as she was for all her brothers and sisters in the art of poetry or the art of life. She wrote once of another being: "There are some creatures, who take / all of history with them / when they kneel one last time / in the hard, bitten grass, / only to come back later / with their sense of life, / their nerve as crisp / as a new apple." Modest as she always was, I'm sure she had no idea she had forged the perfect emblem of her undying spirit.

Her final year was particularly difficult, what with extended bouts of chemo and a month-long stay for bone marrow transplant at the Stanford Medical Center. There had been a brief period of remission—one we measured in weeks not months—and then the resurgence of the illness. I spoke with her on the phone near the end; I'd given her a batch of what to me had been unfamiliar poems by Pavese both in the original Italian and in the new translations by Geoffrey Brock, and she called to thank me for this invaluable gift. Poetry never lost its importance for her, even with the specter of the end only days away. A year ago last spring the community of poets and poetry readers here in the Valley lost one of its guiding stars. We knew then we lost more than a poet: we lost a radiant friend for life who had enriched our years, a woman of independence and spirit whose vision will continue to sing, moving and touching readers for as long as people care about American poetry.

Philip Levine
Fresno, July 2004

PART I

A POEM OF HER OWN

She would like more than
a child's song that
paces slowly backward
into sleep. She wants
a poem of her own—
one that willows over her,
stars and feathers,
a poem with a creature
as small as her finger:
that green Bermudian lizard
whose pulse rippled its
taut skin as it leapt
the torrent of late-day rain
and came to her like
an obedient brother.
The razored shadows of
fern, the snub-nosed
stems of hibiscus
trimmed with machetes—
everything concealed it.
Yet only the steady ladle of
her palm scooped down
to rescue it from the water
percolating on rock.
Wild, fattened on salt,
freckled with limestone,
its frightened soul
paused there for a moment
between heaven and earth
as she held it up and

peered into its eyes
and its puffs of breath
met hers, and neither
by scales nor flesh nor
the last arcs of light
could love be measured.

PALETA

She learned to tie the smudged
wings of her laces and then grasp
her father's long, tanned fingers
with her own small ones before he
heaved his cart across the four lanes
of Belmont Avenue. But the day's
last lesson was reserved for that
moment when the moths had sunk into
the sooty branches of mulberries
and the moon, like a frozen blade,
had begun to slice at the root of
the darkening sky. Then her father
reached into his freezer and
pulled out one paleta by its
pale stick, placing it between
her thumb and forefinger. She had
to balance the weight, the icy
chunks of melon or pineapple
swaying between her open mouth
and the ground beneath her. This
slow dance of gravity her father
taught her until she could suck
the juices up to the tip, staining
her lips like the last band of
sunlight on the leaves and rooftops.
The satin lining of her cheeks
numbed and thawed, and she could
taste the weather of their daily
existence. The neon globes
ripened, swelling into the heavens.
A smaller light came on in their house

as the tin bells on his handrail
announced their arrival, and
his wife stepped out to greet them.
Even then, as the girl slept
on his shoulder, they shared
the day. And her breath
melted the stars of ice, bearing
the scent of mango, banana,
plum—a sweetness
rising from all the empty pockets
this life had given them.

Fifteen years in the blink of an eye,
in the beat of a mother's heart.
Fifteen in the sign of a mustard seed
freed from the charm on her wrist
to the wind. Like a swallow
holding its own in the dark,
bearded skies, Marisela pauses
at the altar—Mother to her left,
Papa to the right and ahead
the priest's long shadow.
The candles sputter and rain
ticks at the amethyst windowpanes.
It is hard to feign seriousness
when she thinks of the saints
on those windows lifting up
their robes to hop the puddles.
Or when the flatted trumpet and
two maracas stir up the wine,
the wafer, the sacred words
like spoons in an old metal pot.
The children fidget on the hard benches
and begin to chitter: has she kissed
her mirror or a second cousin?
Has she nuzzled the cheek
of abuela's old goat?
O, these groomless weddings!
Perhaps, he'll come later with his
shiny black hair and soulful eyes,
fresh from his mother's table.
But, for this one night in eternity,

she is the miracle they've come to see—
in gray shawls tatted by spiders,
in cha-cha skirts and wobbly heels
and hats splayed by sunlight,
cousins from the fields, aunties
on buses all the way from Guadalajara—
this girl whose piety and veiled brow
they've always known, whose arms
as long and brown as theirs
are now a blinding white as she
rises with little more than a wingstroke
and flies out of her childhood.

CONTRABAND

Some come here for grace,
some for the unscented blessing of oil and dust.
But my son has come to Rome to buy cigars
which will turn to powder and blow away
when they meet the dry summer breezes
of California. Sucking in
the fragrant tufts that make him tipsy,
he is also inhaling the ancient breath that
has empowered this city, gilded it,
and given consent to its tobacconists
to charge an arm and a leg for something
that will only go up in smoke.
The aroma is intoxicating. He wants
to take one up between his thumb
and forefinger, examine it reverently
as a boy his age from another country might
study his gun. He wants to press
his shoulders into the warmth of a stucco wall,
waiting in baseball cap and shades for
that moment when the girls on their lunchbreak
gather at the fountain. He imagines
slipping the stout Havana from his breast pocket
like the rolled tongue of a prophet wrapped
in linen and spice. And, snipping off the tip,
he imagines how it will share with him
the secret meaning of the girls' words,
whatever it is he cannot make out
and, most likely, never will.

PROCESSION

She begs to draw the curtain against
the night, keeping out
that glance, deliberate or careless,
the moon's fuzzy eye.
Someone trapped on this earth
desires to touch the walls of this house,
to breathe on its windows and perhaps,
to enter. But to pull that
bright cloth on the darkness would
also swallow the light-to-come.
Soon it will spill into
the chafed branches and blossoms,
into our waking eyes.
It will thrust into the pond,
igniting it. And it will
lighten us just as
the many legs and threaded wings
are making their way upward.
We will join that procession,
throwing off the heart's latch
as the muslin inhales, whispering
there now, you are free to leave.

ADRIFT

Like one of da Vinci's
clam shells, this church came
to a rest on a lip of granite
overlooking the lake.
After the glaciers had
vanished into themselves,
the shifting of continents
slowed to a halt, it settled
here a thousand meters up,
its rosy windows still
perfectly hinged, each
hand-cut Romanesque stone
perched so precipitously
that this morning no one can
leave Mass and wander
aimlessly into the sunlight
without dread of plummeting
to their death. And yet,
this is not about the fear
or the intimate prayers
of the people trapped inside.
If St. Catherine, carved
in oak and painted blue,
could speak, she would point
to the power of speaking
one's mind, to the holiness
stiffening the legs of
an old woman making her way
up the path now, a cane
in one hand, a basket of

greens in the other.
She would praise the steady
spirit of the wind that blows
open the door to the church,
filling the sleeves of each
man, woman, and child so
that they can float slowly
down to their cottages
in the village below.
All in all, words she knows
by heart just as she knows
the taste of bread or
the chill of these stones.
Just as she knows that
other girl, Caterina,
the wool dyer's daughter
who, after the last person
is gone, climbs up to
the roof of the church where
the tile layer is dozing
in the afternoon heat. There
she passes the time with
those who never believed that
the world was flat—the swallows,
the unwavering branches of
the chestnut, a tongue
of smoke rising from the valley.
Still young enough to count
her years, she has no idea
where she'll go next.

But at least beyond those
clouds which, like ashes
or feathers, have been
drifting on the lake since
the beginning of the millennium.

PART II

ELEGY FOR A MATCHMAKER

After the war, the moon
climbed back up and seated
itself on the crest of
a palm tree. Soused on
its own light, it savored
the odd pastiche of fragrances
along the boulevard—lemon
and hot lard, cut grass and
car exhaust until it too
was overcome. The cooling
breeze that made love
possible in the late hours
finally lifted the cloak
of dust off the valley's
shoulders, and all those
nameless stars glistened like
crystal balls. But who
could lift their eyes
to meet the eyes of another,
or to the heavens? No one
from field worker to heat-
drowsed child would even
recall the efforts of
yesterday let alone surrender
to the spells of tomorrow.

So why did Alice Mudirian
and her widowed friends
make such a bother?
On the warmest evenings while

others were out on the town
or propped by windows in
the rooms upstairs, those
three mavens of romance
sipped cups of black tea and
breathed in the scented smoke
spewing from a metal cone
on the kitchen table.
They broke *lavosh* in their
sweaty palms and chattered
away in words unpacked
from battered suitcases
a generation ago. And then,
they danced—arm in arm,
the weaving steps too sprightly
for their thickened knees—
calling up lost loves
of forty years before.
Summoning the spirits of
men in spats and bowlers,
uniformed tenors, even
barechested boys who
only required a few moments
on earth to make good old
promises. Enough to fill
the shadowed parlor and
startle the sleeping
boarders. Enough to keep
the balalaika weeping.

Summer after summer,
the matchmakers' dreams
were the nightmares of
young girls. The three were
getting old, their dances
sluggish, the florid
pattern in the Persian rug
now a muted cloud of
broken threads. It had
come to the point where
any pair would do, any two
who were willing to toss
the dust and weeds of
their own hearts into
the night air. It was less
carelessness than desperation
if a lanky gentleman
appeared on the porch at
sundown, nervously clutching
a bouquet for the girl
upstairs in her seventh month,
her belly swollen like
a ship's hull ploughing those
invisible waves of heat.
And so, the moon spilled its
light for the spiked fronds
to lap up. And a truck driver
alone with his coffee on
the #99 corridor felt
a strange affection for

the crates of tomatoes
he bore on his dolly
night after night. Even
Mrs. Mudirian clasped her
houserobe at the throat and
acknowledged the vacant
gaze of Mr. Torosian probing
the sidewalk with a cane.
The rest of us? Upon
hearing the warped strains
of that long-dead Armenian
songbird rise up through
the floorboards, the cracked
windows, we sat on the edge
of our beds and caught
our breath, blessing our
hard-earned solitude
before falling back to sleep.

THE KISS

I go to close the shutters on a night
that will not darken or silence itself.
Wine glasses, bell chimes, street sweepers
go on singing without me.
Stooped in the shadows, he gazes up at me
from his bench on the piazza
and blows me a kiss.
Suddenly, a bird swoops down and
scours the ground under the empty café tables.
Perhaps, a dove from the countryside.
Perhaps, a sign of his death or
mine. But the streetlamp blossoms
on the paving stones and no one
can see that the kiss has risen.
Risen not to the heavens,
but as close as you can get from here—
the third floor of #26 della Rotunda
where it slips through the thick
wooden slats and, with the kindness of
a stranger, enters my room.

OVERTURES

My husband sleeps serenely to
the manic strains of Russian overtures.
Mussorgsky's hussars leap from
the crowded closet of his dreams,
stomping that rare, but pleasing grace note
slipped in from the countryside.
Next door, in the grip of a death-green kitchen,
they're singing to old 78s
brought up from Guadalajara. She
soaps the coffee cups in the sink
while he, sitting behind her, stammers
off-key *ay'eeee*s, never taking his
eyes off her supple backside where
the apron strings fall—all longing,
little action. The dancing is
taking place at a new bar a block away
where low-riders stack their cars
like dominos. Their swagger
is poison. Their bass rumbles up
through the legs of alley cats.
And no one surrenders when
the cops arrive, sirens warbling
like old saws. Will I ever
get to hear again the rain, the wind
drubbing the walls of our house?
They say it is gone forever, the slow rhythm
that once carried us from night into day,
no matter how softly the old man
taps his cane on the floor or
how many times his wife resets the needle
and turns to sing just to him,
rolling her eyes up to the heavens.

AIN'T MISBEHAVIN'

If Willie the Lion Smith
walked into this room
this very moment
like the notes of his music
striding over us,
would he feel at home?
The same old fan wobbling on
its one bad leg, a lamp
to lob his hat over,
the same summer storm at 2 A.M.,
dampening the matching silks,
the new cigar. 1934,
and all the clubs in Atlantic City
are boarded up. A man needs
a place he can go and
let out a sigh after
a night on the keys.
What are we missing?
A set of ivories in the corner,
as black and white as
our bodies stretching
their octaves, one
bending under the other
as the shafts of rain
pool on the sills. *Will you*
come to me, will you—
in Richmond, in Paris?
No matter the weather.
In mellisonant shadows,
the Lion bears down and finds
his rhythm, whispering *yes.*

THE ESCAPE

Luzmila's been careless again—
her roosters have wandered
into the road and their cries
are shredding the moonlight.
Even in sleep our ears suffer
the repetition. Like waves
gnawing sand or gusts of wind
that squeal in the eaves,
they can't seem to get it right.
From everywhere, the sound
draws mongrels with glowing eyes
into a half-circle on the curb.
It pushes lovers closer together
so they wake with an elbow
in the rib and each other's
breath on their lips.
It straightens the branches
of the trumpet vine whose
blossoms bleat their dirge
for the darkened world.
Finally, the sun crawls
bravely over the eastern shelf,
spreads her arms and coaxes
them homeward. To a hutch
under the clothesline where
sleeves shrug and a hen
dozes on two stained eggs.
The morning which Luzmila
and the rest of us greet is

as silent as any stranger
who tells his story and flees,
dropping behind him a fan of
ragged feathers on the wet grass.

CHARENTAIS

As with love, good food
should take its time.
And so the clouds formed
slowly over the hills
and sparrows nibbled the last
patches of light. Hunger
overtook that small café
until the sun's final
gleaming ray slipped through
the rind of charentais,
splitting it open on
the platter before you.
All eyes turned from
their bowls of soup and
thinly sliced paté when
a waiter stepped forth
from the shadows, tipped
his bottle and filled
the tender melon pockets
with the blood-red liquor.
No one was left unmoved
by that beauty, the day's
fire gathered up in
a single spoon. Then
the sun went down and
a couple kissed across
their table. A few seeds
floated to the surface.
The white cloths were
folded up like stars into

the darkened sea. And
sparrows took to the street
in a serious tango.

                *

Thirteen years, and I
still remember the braid
of sugar on our tongues.
After a miracle, you learn
how to pull your chair
away from the table and
stand for a moment
over the empty plates,
silent and humble. And
later that night, in a room
above the kitchen's clamor,
you come together to taste
again the lingering flavor—
flesh, cassis. Below,
it's metal to metal,
bone into broth, glass
into air, the endless alchemy
of a love-starved chef who
douses the light, slaps
his towel on the thigh of
a tired kitchen girl and
goes out into the alley
where all aromas blend into
one: charentais, rosemary,
scallion. From the distance,

he hears the heavy stomach
of the sea, but wonders if
the groaning could be from
those in the rooms above.
In love, as it is with good
food, there will always be
some who can never get enough.

ATONEMENT

What punishment awaits
the person who hurls a weed
into his neighbor's yard?
Or even worse—a second and
a third because the ground is
soft from rain, the flinging
easy, back-handed and up
over the crouched haunches
like a mule kicking dirt.
Much worse—clumps of
crabgrass fettered with mud
and families of beetles
sailing silently through
pure air into exile.
I know that wherever
they land, they will hook
their long toes, hunker down
and creep back over
when my head is turned.
In Dante's mucky chambers,
I would be the soul buried
thigh-deep for eternity,
sorting silt from root,
never to see or grasp again
the fresh greens sprouting
behind me. Or the one
with cheek to mulch, forced to
witness the difficulties
of subterranean intercourse.
And what becomes of the person
who, when weeding is done,

the beds made clean, rakes
with a frenzy as though
the sky had fallen or
the carcass of a bluejay
wrapped in leaves would make
them whorl once more.
Defrocked of his feathers, his
chatter stolen long ago
by stray cats, what makes me
think that there is still
a judgment left in him?
Let the twilight bring
peace to his frail bones,
to the fading rose, to these
palms scored with earth.
And peace to the neighbor who
proudly measures the milkweed
pushing up into the empty
branches of his apple tree.

BY CANOE

When you push us off
the mesh of grass and sand,
we enter the current
like a needle. I've seen
lace as fine before,
the soft backcurl of foam
on glittery darkness.
In the hem of a dress
my mother wore to a dance
one summer night where
a drunk priest made
a pass at her. Because
this is the same river
that carried moonlight over
those dancers many years ago,
and because no one has
seen him since, I search
for his face in the shifting
depths, among the branches
and rusted fenders.

Growing up in this valley,
I felt deprived of water,
the glint and spill of
the just-beyond. As we
glide south, then slowly
westward, I drag my fingers
through the swollen wake,
filling the silence
with strange translations
from the river bottom.

Suddenly, a heron appears
before us, unfazed by
the glare of field crows.
Then he lifts and vanishes
into the shadows where
willows tangle easily
with the splayed black oak.
On the bank, the cows
dip their noses into
the sage, the thistle
sags in the dust. And
the river-ghosts breathe
a sigh as we go on—
featherweight,
wind-blown, unstoppable.

PART III

STAR GAZERS

They are the least stable of all men—
those connoisseurs of heavenly light,
their shoes dipped in the evening dew,
their fingers white and arched.
And the proud, black cylinder
angles into the northern skies where
twin stars burst like a seam
in the dark. The first in line
is a child who tries to fly into
that darkness, but misses his step.
As he reaches out, the giant lens
swings around, whirling down past
the pocked orbs and ghostly nimbus
into the realm of our gases,
soot, and the rays of our budding
houselamps. When the scope's gaze
finally lands, we can see the flaring
boughs of a jacaranda, and it seems
that the stars of this earth are
falling on us. While some of us
are seized by a sudden flightiness,
others have learned to stay cool
and turn to stone on such occasions.

                    *

When we were first lovers,
we neither soared nor froze
but gathered up the fragments of stars
along with the chunks of gravel,
glass, and thorn, then smoothed the dust

and made a bed for ourselves on
the floor of an abandoned water tower.
Through the vast hole where the roof
might have been, the sky poured in on us
the fragrance of the orchards and all
the small lights dancing above
at arm's length. We traded places,
staring up at the sky or down
into each other's face while, beyond
our walls, a brighter crescent
etched the hubs of tractors parked
in the fields for the night.

*

O, how those nervous men and their small boats
batter the waves of the cosmos...
back and forth over the luminous swells.
Some shipwreck on the lethal prongs
of stars. Some imagine themselves adrift
in a huge pot of boiling broth and
think that if they could only lift the lid,
they would find the source of light,
the slow flame that warms this soup.
But the oldest astronomer waits
patiently for it to cool. And though
his body is knitted to the night,
he seldom sleeps, but flips through
pages where there is no mention of love.
He has begun to see rings everywhere—
on water or matted grass or

in the glow of fruit resting in
the orchard dust. And he is troubled
by our passion for things held down
by gravity, and by how that passion
warms both our fingertips and breath.

EMISSARY

The first thin smile of moonlight
since Christmas. Three men,
neither wise nor gifted,
who remember the gasp of birth
as though it were yesterday,
huddle at the corner of Fourth
and Divisadero. One drags
a bicycle missing a tire,
another clutches a sack of bread
and the third gestures wildly,
slapping the cold air. All
three wear trousers stained with
the dark soil of the same two
countries, and all three pocket
a crust for later. A crow,
fueled on trash, spirals
downward over the Texaco station
and laughs at those below
who would work for food.
Laughing back, one of the men
imagines how they would look
gliding on its back for
a landing in the middle of
Avenida de la Revolución,
the citizens of that vast city
stunned with awe. And then,
to save themselves, they go
their separate ways. For
not one of them has learned
to ride a unicycle, and not one

has enough to buy the others
a drink. And only one knows
a woman with a large bathtub
not far from here. Leaping into
the crosswalk, he waves at
the ladies as he passes
their cars: emissary of crow,
bearing word of the bitten field,
the starless sky, whose heart
still crackles and whose gut
is wrestling with moldy bread.

THE GYPSY

A full moon shrouds the cathedral,
spilling over the saints
and swollen buttresses. She wears
no veil as she paces the steps,
and you can see her smile
rise like Lazarus as she struts
from one man to another, thrusting
her palm under their noses.
She makes it plain she only wants
lira notes—for herself and
the child, of course, coiled
in the fluted hem of her skirt.
And perhaps a few for the man
left behind in the countryside.
Unlike the others who cross
themselves as they pass through
the carved doors, she bares
her shoulders to the world of men,
shrugging at their gifts. She
cares neither for the shy student
who shows her the holes in his pockets,
nor for the dapper Torinese who
flicks her aside with his cane.
She is quicker than the rest,
than the chosen twelve
painted at supper over the apse
by Michelangelo. While they
are bowing their heads. She could
grab the bread off their finely
laid table, never breaking the spell,

never minding the crumbs that fly
into the warm summer night as she
runs full-speed for the freight yard.

GOOD MEN

The slow, blue shadows of the olive groves
follow the workers back into town.
Like patches, the shadows cling
to the sweaty folds of their shirts
and trousers. But the men imagine
something else has weighed them down,
like hunger or the day's heat
or a weariness so deep that
even love could never reach them.

Yet the sashes of darkness curl in
the dust around each trunk.
They are as blue as the shadows
under the eyes of a woman
whose picture lies crumpled on
the floor of the garage where
the men sleep: elbow to thigh,
toe to skull, they seldom
roll into dream or dare to
think of delicate nails
dragging their inky stain across
the shoulder of moonlight.

When I've seen them at dusk,
tracing the threads of gravel in
their last, few steps
down the alley, hunched over,
their swollen knuckles
shoved into pockets, I've wanted to
call to them to forget the olive,

the sagging plum, the worm nestling on
the balconies of rotted bark,
and stand up straight.

But their boss has already told them
what good men they are—
Preciliano, Jorge, and Cantú
with a few black nuggets
rolled up in his cuff.
The boss's wife appears with
piles of tortillas that will soak up
the day's shadows and banish
their hunger. And tomorrow,
these *good men* will go out once more
to kneel under the branches and
pry off fruit whose firm,
bitter flesh never falls
willingly into the palm.

FLIERS

He was twenty-eight,
with eyes as dark as the rain
that night, hair dampened
and parted slowly by
a finger of blood.
We were told that he had
gone from house to house,
knocking. But no one answered.
And so he knocked on other doors—
the blackbird's, the squirrel's.
And when there was still
no answer, he climbed
his way up, arm over arm,
into the branches, looking
for something, a stem
or a star to ease his hunger,
a whorl of bark to cradle him.
Higher and higher, until
he thought he could
hear the voices of birds
and tried to call out,
to follow. We did not
know him, and yet men are
always falling to earth.

*

At dawn, my son dips his small face
into the basin of water and,
with both palms, attempts to
flatten the crown of skewed curls.
He announces to the mirror,

which agrees with everything
he says, that he is going
to be a flier, a master of currents:
F-14s, B-24s, Spitfires,
Phantoms. He lists
the wings he will guide
and others which don't exist.
All the wars with their
glorious nosedives, smoky
trails and infinite deaths
swirl into one in that head
which he covers now with
a Dodgers cap as he darts
into the sunlight and vanishes.

*

Some wings fail while others
rise, second-by-second
through the rosy filaments of
the day's first light.
Perhaps, I should do what
men would do in the last war,
raising their glasses
as they waited for the names
of those who were missing
to come to their lips:

Here's to the grazer of treetops,
the bullier of crows,
to the one who hurled a bottle
out of the cockpit window

and the other who blew
his nose into the clouds, knowing
it had a fifty-fifty chance of
reaching the trenches below.
And here's to the one who
came back to find no one home,
the houses banked like
weathered arks, the earth
washed by a steady rain, and
his wings asleep on his shoulder
like a useless angel who
has lost its love for the wind.

THE WINDOW

Mike (so-called because
America swallowed
the r's of Mardiros),
pinches a nail between
his lips and squints into
the pale glass. Over the sink,
a huge, impeccable square
in a cedar frame to catch
both the piercing light
and the slightest changes
in season. He has hammered
the roaches out of the walls,
robins out of the locust trees,
and driven the neighbor's dog
so crazy that it curls up
silently in the presence
of cats and darkness.
But with the first glint of
day, we can see more than
we'd ever imagined: the buds
of quince and pear, pigeons
breaching the tall grass,
lemons thrashed by sunlight.
Anyone passing our house can
find himself in this window.
When a truck pulls to the curb,
neither bread nor morning milk,
but a rig from the highway,
it rumbles as though to
awaken these small houses

and recapture the string of
trilled letters a man might need
on a journey from one world
to another. We watch as
the driver climbs from the cab
and gathers a few sprigs—
violets, feathers, whatever
small gesture he can find for
a woman hours ahead.
Like her, I return once more
to test the sill, to graze
the glass with my fingers.
And to measure the air itself,
the lulls and shimmers repeating
their praise for the men
who have laid the whole of this
tongue-tied country at our feet.

PART IV

COMINGS AND GOINGS

Field after field, the masks of
alkali repeat themselves,
rags snap in the wind,
and Russian thistle roll
like heads through the dust.
It could take years to
reach the far edges of this
valley, a lifetime to
get to the cities just beyond.
One autumn at dawn, this
ran through her mind as
Miss Emily Murray pressed
her broad foot to the gas and
whisked her four star
pupils of public speaking
out of the flatlands toward
the Championship, San Francisco,
1939. And their young voices,
primed and burnished like
the finish on her Model A,
would bravely carve
their futures elsewhere.

Such comings and goings,
they used to say to make
sense of the way an automobile
could take you anywhere and
have you back before nightfall.
In the cool, dark corridors
of my grandfather's garage, I
tallied the bolts and gaskets

while outside the heat of
August stopped others dead in
their tracks. Each lugnut
was worthy of its journey,
each streak of carbon on
the fractured, sunlit panes
like a shadow of a cloud
on a freshly turned field.
Whose goings, I wondered,
for any departure from that
small town seemed miraculous.
The wheeze of air hoses
scattered the pigeons from
the rafters, and an engine
that had gurgled at daybreak
idled peacefully now at
the back of the garage.
5 p.m., the men threw down
their rags and wrenches, took
their blackened hands and tired
souls home to their wives.

When the screen door slammed,
my grandmother, who had been
left with three children,
a yard full of animals and
one new Dodge, barely
noticed the neighbor panting
behind her with news, but
breathed in the kettle's vapors,
blotted the berry stains on

her fingers, and removed
the long-handled spoon. Then
she turned to listen:
Miss Emily Murray, with all
of her noble intentions,
was no good behind the wheel.
Even my grandfather said
she had come to both men
and cars too late in life.

Dust devil, puddle, a patch of
grease—whatever it took—
sent her wheels spinning
sunward, and that gleaming
bucket of standardized parts,
hand-rubbed chrome rolling
into the loam and muck of
a pasture. The miracle then:
one boy sneezing through
the aura of haydust,
another wiping the oil on
his knickers, and Miss Murray,
who could never be anything
less than a teacher, reaching
for the roll sheet, calling
each by name. Even the one
caught in the tangle of
arms and legs, laughing not
out of the terror of her driving
or the joy of survival, but
at a cow upside-down, outside

his window, chewing on one of
those stiff, yellow flowers—
both plant and animal taking
root, to hell with the future,
knowing well that the walk
back home was much too long.

A NEST FOR EVERYONE

The possum with four crazed paws
and a mouthful of broken teeth
is too old to brave the highway
again for a chase that blurs
into flight. The cold morning sun
grazes the husks of November,
the shoulders of workers crouched
between vines. They lower
their knives, the bronzed
leaves fall to the mud, and
the fluttering stops for a moment.
Then a wave of crows ascends
from a furrow, each bearing in
its beak a token of the season—
a flailing worm, a wisp of straw,
the strip of an old sleeve
that once bound an arm or
a shattered brow and still has
the fiery stain to show for it.

Last night, this side of a steamy,
blackened window, my children
wanted to believe that there
must be a nest for everyone.
As my son struck a match, the soft
wick of the candle flared into
a prayer for our survival.
It is the dead of winter and
vines are fluted with darkness,
wired to wooden stakes. It will
take all eight candles to cast

the light of their small faces
on the glass. And many more
than that to warm all the cupped
hands waiting not far beyond.

This month, the man who holds
the deed to this gnarly orchard and
that parcel of sleeping grass
is moving slower. Hours pass,
the rows of numbers won't bear fruit.
He leans back on his chair and
stares up at the empty sky of
his kitchen ceiling. Whatever
fluttered into the fields will
go back the way it came:
birds, leaves, the endless
bleating of the neighbor's bull,
even the workers themselves
quickly dividing limb from sky,
and the stars that will rise soon
over this valley. They will all
go back to the schemes of earth
and air, like those wild nests
left vacant in winter, embracing
the light, letting some of it go.

THE MUTINY OF ANGELS

Had you awakened later as the full flush
of light lifted the flowers from
the pale stitches of your quilt, had you
felt the strength of a good night's sleep,
you might have fought them off.
But, on the twenty-third day of wind,
you turned in your last dream
to face the silver branches slashing
the empty spaces the sky would fill—
the mutiny of angels had begun
and no one could stop it. For weeks,
their numbers had grown in the grubby
corners of this city until the scorched
lilacs thrashing the fences teemed
with celestial cousins. And with no
respect for your need to return
gracefully to the earth, to that new day
after a night of frightful journeys,
they took to the alleys in robes
hopelessly patched and bleached
like the first renegade rays.
They banged on lids and peeked into
the bedroom window where your wife
was just stretching and rubbing her
half-opened eyes. And from each
soft sputter, each hard-earned
breath of the man beside her, more
angels were released into the air.
Throughout the days, they made
circles around us like streams of
small foreign cars; they scrapped and

shoved like the crows who had stolen
the most majestic branches in the sycamores.
They followed the rows of ants up
the trunks of orange trees, into
the fragrance that drifted out like
a voice carried by the wind. At dusk,
on that twenty-third day of wind,
the sky was finally still, and the dust
that settled on leaves and porches
also clung to the tender sills of
our eyes. We were unable to tell if
our tears were from wonder or pain.
The angels had taken what they wanted
and left. They had taken you.
I stood at the sink, tamped out
wings of garlic and watched them
flutter as they slid into
the skillet. Let these be
the last two angels to touch
your tongue—the bitter clove
and the white star of the orange,
one for the beauty of tears
and one for the fire we must
fly into and dance with.

Ernesto Trejo, 1950–1991

VA A STRESA *

The monk cradles a bundle of peonies
in his left arm,
breast-pink blossoms
bobbing as he pedals hard
up the gravelly road.
Today, the spokes are shadowless,
spinning like pinwheels
as heaven approaches. Or, at least,
comes a thousand feet closer
if the bureau of transportation
has done its math.
And maybe twice that, since
he has given his only cigarette
to an old man on foot—
nobody's son and nobody's father
but, like Aesop's tortoise,
waiting at the summit
to welcome him. He wonders if
these flowers will survive
the journey, their petals
leaving a bright trail
on the rain-splotched road.
Or the mighty column
of summer ants marching
beside him with no particular
fate assigned to them.
Surely, the dry, feathery grass
on the roadside has already
entered the next world
and is just returning

   *Go to Stresa

for a visit, on loan
as it were. The doubts
that come with exhaustion
are both spiritual and
mechanical. Is it possible
that a bicycle could be
one's final vehicle of faith?
But then, a curve and
a spasm of pure light, the pale
muscle of a full moon:
he has finally arrived!
Breathless from swallowing
clouds all day, a fire
rises up through his calves
and a cold sweat beads his cheeks
like the tears of a sparrow.
And who would believe
this scene? Under an elm,
a table set with bread
and a glass. A breeze ripples
the pages of the day's news
as though nothing had happened.
And an old hound lounges
on the cold stone step
inhaling…exhaling, with
that dogged smile of gratitude
you only see in heaven.

ESCAPING SAVONAROLA

They say his voice was thin,
his speech rutted
like a country path as he
damned them all, promising
a place for their souls
as small and dark as
an old woman's thimble.
No wonder they fled,
even the bravest Florentine,
if only to their gardens
outside the walls where
the sunflower and fennel
swayed peacefully. For
pleasure was everything.
The flood of his fearful words
must have quickened
their pace, some fleeing
even further with their casks
of wine and feather bedding
to the starry meadows
of Futa Pass. There,
like raven and wren,
they nestled together
and the cries of hell
seemed far away.

                *

Witchgrass, lavender,
shadowy pockets of birch
and pine, each gentle

curve up the hillside brings
the relief of rising
above it all. I peer down
from a bluff on the small
fires of men flaring in
the city below: bright
ribbon of the autostrada,
emberous streetlamps
wreathing the squares where
once the pyres of books,
false hair and meters
of red satin smouldered
and were swept away.
At the summit, a small café
and a few survivors who
still remain. The old men
bent over an endless game
of cards turn to us with
the only question they can
remember: not, *Are they saved?*
but, *Is he dead yet?*

And, *Can they go home?*
Yes…and no, I think,
eyeing the pig splayed on
the marble counter where
a girl is assembling
my sandwich. The braised
sow hoards in her lumberous
folds the true secret of

transcendence: a blind eye
and an indifference to air
which makes passion possible.
Save your breath, the sow
might say to those men grumbling
over a card up the sleeve,
a pot missing lire. They
would never believe that
just a few steps from where
they once lived, the ashes
mounding into pyramids,
the paving stones were now
streaked with burnt rubber.
Or that in the rooms
along the river, the threats
had conceded to the silence
of the singed tongue. Now,
a fragrance rose: garlic,
tobacco, cologne.
Their old rooms in which
the chairs and tables waiting
patiently over the years
had finally given up,
knowing as the window knew
with its gaze on those
distant peaks that once
they ascended, they would
never come back down.

THE VIGIL

I have seen them watching over us, settling
in the clouds above: my grandmother,
after her century on this earth,
in the arms of her husband who has waited
since the blackened skies of '36.
And generations of housecats
vexed by the white vapors of sparrows;
prize fighters pummeling the green
hillsides in spring; blossoms
my children offered up
in their grass-stained palms,
blooming a second time overhead.

One loss billows out of another as
we remember how each spirit flies
like spit off the tongue.
Nimbus, stratus, cirro-velum,
the ancients knew them all.
They scattered salt to calm
the storms of the heavens and the flesh.
As a child, my grandmother sat
on the rain-splotched steps
and called up to her grandfather, McCracken,
in the skies over Pittsburgh
to send down another gold coin
as proof of his presence.
And he let it fly, the pellets
of hail gleaming as they
slipped into her shoes and melted.

Whom should I call to now,
the thrush or the pine bough
swallowing the mist? To the voice
which has left the lips of those
we loved and been orphaned in mid-air?
We slip from the cloud's grasp
as they drift south, leaving us behind.
Yet, even on days when the sky
weighs as much as a body being lowered,
there is a light between the stripped branches,
a radiance leaping off the bark,
and a stream of rain running to the end
of each twig, dropping into an emptiness
that seems to breathe again.

FROM *SILKS* (1980)

BUILDING A SMALL HOUSE

In the dream that pulls
me to the wall, a chill
rises from the mortar.
I watch carpenters perched
over the bare frame,
insects sailing
between the studs. An old man
carrying a bucket of plaster
moves toward me;
another measures
doorways wide enough
for diesels and clouds.

I can't understand
how these men keep
themselves in my dream.
I refuse to be the nail
that holds this place together.

        *

In the old books
the carpenter shows up
before dawn, breaking
bread in his favor
with a silent partner.
The two watch women
dump garbage from the windows
and know that each village
has a genius who dies in bed,
but are never asked
for an opinion.

At the end of the day
they wipe their hands
on their undershirts
and vanish,
like air between the pages.

*

When I wake
there is a vein
of light on the shade.
They have left me
a soft foundation
under sheets imprinted
by children's hands,
and you who still hang high
in sleep, like a crane,
and can build
without lifting a finger.

Our imperfections
show up now—blotches
like rusty nails,
knots bored in sleep.
The earth shifts
inside of me:

When I was young
my father raised walls
of steam in the bathroom
and walked through them,
but came back each night
to disappear again.

*

Later the alley will rumble,
flies storm the trash.
The hammering begins.

Tract of lids, waxed peel
carved by blunt teeth,
shingle of fur—what I make
will be nameless.
A neighbor watches the apron
bulging at my waist
and spreads her sheets
on the line between us.
At dusk, her son will be
waiting in the shadows
to help me carry the tools.

THE FIDDLER'S WIFE

Late at night
my husband plays the fiddle
by a candle in his study.
His eyes are heavy
and he is always learning.
Pumping has thickened his right arm
as autumn has the evening air
with its blendings of smoke
and color, and nothing
interrupts him—

not the copper chimes
turned by the wind,
nor the sound of his own heart.

Shadows steal the spindled notes
before they reach me in my sleep
many rooms away,
and what I finally hear is darkness

breaking in my body,
a fine tune.

                    *

I can't decide if its rosy flanks
remind me of a man's or a woman's.
Those who've shouldered this angel
through a gallant reel
have lived in neither world:
the blind fiddler who feels the breeze
of a woman's skirt, the one with a nose so big

he must cock his head to the right
to receive his own music, the drunkard
surviving below all vibrations.

These though are the masters.
Their secrets are the rosin
drained from the oldest trees,
a loneliness that undresses itself
again and again.

                    *

You tell me the story of Stradivari
who must have left his own wife before dawn
to pace the empty docks
as the bow of a merchant ship
was dredged from the pale water.

You explain the mystery of mahogany
cured in brine,
urchin-stained, the pitch
of oxygen trapped in this perfect wood.

If Antonio got his bargain
in the mellow curve and vibrato
of a flowering world, he also
loaded his heart onto this vessel
that now carries you away.

At sunrise
he returned to his bed,
remembering the delicate slits,

the dark veneer of a mouth
that never closes…

*

I should have known when I married
a man who plays the fiddle…

In the shadows
I can see the shape of my hand.
Its fingers, too small and uncallused,
mean nothing at my own task.

I should have known on that first night,
in the kitchen
lit by a single bulb,
when the music of seven men
ran the color of whiskey
and I learned that the finest strings
come from the guts of a cat.

But what can I say
when I only knew how to sing it,
the high wail of Appalachia
caught in the back of the throat,
as we left the house
for the cool air of the country
where it all began,
arm in arm,
the eyes of stars on us.

THE WHITE DRESS

I want you to see me in it.

The mirror witches an image
that invents every movement. When I spin
I enter the seven precious stages of flight;
the room is as lively as a dovecote.
Again I turn and stop,
looking into your eyes
where the feathers are drifting down
over my thighs and knees.
The cloth obeys the curves of my body.
It is as simple as this,
a white dress.

Later we will leave the party and walk
the cool sidewalks toward the highway
where junipers nod in the wind.
When my skirt ripples out into darkness
you will move me, like a sail
in its first gentle breaths
toward the open sea. White
is a mixture of many understandings.

The bare arm,
the angle of fiber on skin,
two thin strings at the neck
undoing the world…
Now turn away.

Sunlight is living in the storefront window
and the shopkeeper wants her money.
I want your opinion

years from now
when you've forgotten how I look in white.

CONSIDERING FIRE

I try to name
the last noises,
the possibilities of danger
while I sleep:
the asthmatic singing
of our neighbor's girl,
summer wind sugaring
the dry leaves, cars a mile off
down the main road,
a man's empty clothes.

As a child
I dreamed that fire would send me
out into the damp grass,
the singed curtains drifting
through the windows—
into morning, the cotton tatters
hooked in the upper branches
of mulberries along the block.
But this new house is cement:
the paint smudges,
the nails give.
Once the laboratory of a doctor,
our bedroom is the recovery room
where the floors drain—
it is so sound
that nothing happens.

Throwing shadows
across my legs, the sheet
unrolls like a list

of what to take or leave:
the person sleeping next to me,
too heavy to carry,
my cactus pregnant
in its tin pot,
the words of certain friends—
the little fires
that burn anywhere.

THINGS MOST OFTEN
LEFT BEHIND

1

The easy lacework of the streetlight
and leaves on the blackened window—
a vision beautiful and frightening.
Our neighbor stands on his porch
staring out into the night,
preserving a secret he'll take
to his grave. His pipe smoke
drifts up through the telephone wires
to the moon that wears it
like a nightgown. He taps
the tiny bowl on his palm
and the dark flakes scatter,
the last seeds of a man.

2

To say he knows it will rain
would not be true; or that he sees
his own muddy tracks on the sidewalk
before daylight; to say he hears
the party of nameless birds
chattering under the wooden eaves
of his house in anticipation
would be foolish.
He simply needs something to cover him,
something less than the sky,
but more than the woman he's never had,
or closer to him than a house.
A shelter for someone just his size.

At the door, an umbrella is sleeping wisely—
will it open its wings
and be found again?

3

Then finally the rain falls
like teeth biting the earth;
and when he dies,
we stand over him grinning
unaware of how we look.
Teeth are the last thing to be forgotten,
because in the end food is soft
and the breath falters further down.
Even now, his shine through the hard layers
as he smiles back at us,
knowing his secret is well hidden.

DUST

for Elizabeth Cotton

I know that it comes from the ground,
the jittery skin of hardpan.
But *oh* how the wind seems to own it,
making it rise and move through us
though we'd swear we'd seen nothing.

When I was a young woman
he took me to the cemetery on Saturdays
where we spread out
under a few toothless oaks
to stare down in silence at the valley
baking in the afternoon.
I smoothed my yellow skirt
into its own valleys
where he put his head and slept,
so happily. I still don't shudder
when I think of the dead.

See how it masks the faces of this valley,
how it makes the chard and bluegrass
rattle like ghosts.
See how one sparrow becomes two
that never age, how the eyes
wall up and the tongue thickens.
Folks have to take the train
to get back to where they belong.
I've run through dust
trying to reach the love in you
and found an early grave.

This is why I sing.
My voice is the fist of gravel
children fling at an old woman.
I pick up the broom,
beat the step, and laugh at dust
so they'll know I'm still alive.

THE TRAVELER

for Peter

At the edge of the village,
battered stalks and then a field
of poppies. You drop your pack
to the ground, picking
the few that will last
until you find others.

Among the stalks,
an old farmer
whose plow has died.
Wearing these flowers
you remind him of his son
who let the fields
go to seed. Not everyone
will be quick to claim you:

you're a foreigner—
American—maybe a Messiah
whose gray hairs mingle
with the clouds,
and even slightly girlish
with the poppies swaying
behind one ear.

Later, you see men
like him again and again:
their shadows on dry grass,
their hats left on village walls,

and you want to call them
by name…
                    But in the fields
the petals are stained glasses
filling quickly with sunlight
and dust; you tap the last dirt
from the roots and go on.

STORY

I

Weighted with snow,
the hemlock branches
hang to the ground.
To keep from dreaming
the mare drags her tail
through the swollen needles
and powders the air,
then backs up
butting her hooves
until the chips of ice
fall away.

At dark, old winter-woman
speaks into the mare's ear,
gives her a slice of moon
that looks like a carrot,
and leads her gently
over the mountain—
they never come back.

We ask the cold for directions,
but it is silent.
The screech of the road salter
carries for miles—
the deer flinch,
the river remembers
her husband who drank
all summer.

We climb the mountain,
following the tracks
of an animal threaded
through those of a snowmobile.

Winter,
infiltrator of soft linings,
perfect tooth of stone,
thief of horses
and children…
When we call, our voices
turn and come meekly
back to us.

2

Rain washes one county
into the next,
mud over bones
and matted branches of hemlock.
No trace of the familiar,
there is no chance
of finding something
that was lost the month before.

The curves in the trail
now lead to a pool
of lost ice, the rocks
sleep together,
their mouths hanging open,
the smooth hindquarters

of the mountain are mulched
with needles and ground fern.

But we are young enough
to watch the old woman
bury her mask
and make her getaway:

she is the screech owl
that falls to the road,
like a rock,
frightening the deer,
the skull of the mare
that flapped off in the breeze.

THE TREES BEGAN TO SPEAK

I

The trees began to speak and this frightened her,
deep chanting fir
using the lips of those she knew.
When the sky darkened and the air cooled
the voices became clearer.
There were twice as many stars
as ever before. In her heart,
a valley where there were no trees
and the sky kept to itself.

She had always been known
for peeking into the lives of others,
for throwing the windows open
to let the million fearsome insects
float off in the breeze.
She was also known for dancing in strong winds
that showed her real strength.

If you've seen a skirt of dust
whirl down from the Sierra
and heard the rag jangled out
on the keyboard of scrub and pine
you're probably a distant relative.

She will visit you soon.

2

By morning
the mountains were covered with people.
The sunlight made it clear who they were—
those lugging pails of water uphill,
children scampering over the beds of needles
as though there were no mountains.

Across the lake
men snoozed under blankets of hair
and swamp grass; three women
entered the water in perfect harmony.
She couldn't hear what they were saying,
but could see their lips move
and feel the ringing in her bones.

3

Oarlock screwed into splintered wood,
paddle nudging the sandy shoal,
the boat came toward her…

She dressed in the shadows of redwoods,
she stirred the ashes with dust and lake water,
counting the carbonous specimens,
the late moments of solitude
before it arrived.

It mattered less that the boat was empty
than where it would take her.

4

So what if trees spoke?
She had listened too carefully.
It was good that they had their secret language.
They shouldn't remind you of a friend
giving advice, or your old aunt
warning you to stay away from a certain man.
They shouldn't make you think
of ancestors pacing the earth,
drawling the stories you heard as a child.
They shouldn't make you think of yourself.

The boat was built from the wood
of trees brought closer to earth
by the wind, the wind braiding
the light in the branches,
in the wings of a wading bird
who had the world to himself.

This was the last time she would see
her body rise like a trunk
through the seasons of water
and remember everything
she had ever learned.

TONSILS

I

Two seahorses smiled at me
from a glass of water on the nightstand,
two wishbones of the speech

I wished for.
There were two pink and fibrous roots
picked from a forest

or were they my mother's fingers
pressed twice their size
as she held the glass for me to drink?

I remember it perfectly
though the hospital danced in fog
at 4 A.M.

I was dressed in the blues
of an absent child, to be undressed
by those in gray

calling me back to sleep.
And I swam back, like the small horses,
through the sheets of foam

and water with land on all sides.
The blade trimmed,
mahogany walled and drifted,
glass held water.

2

The hospital is gone,
the rows of small windows sucked out
and scattered over a foundation

that leads back to earth.
Nearly everyone is missing something.
But few remember the colors

or the silence that pushes us away
from its world.
This is a memory of beginnings,

of creatures more exotic
than redworms or stunned flies.
It is to be spoken without swallowing:

a memory painless
as a hen's bone broken for a second time
on a new wish, as a root

lifted gently from the mud,
or clear water
without a name for it.

SILKS

1 The Silk Maker

He lives in the same house with the worms,
and his fingers are the first to touch their heavens.

In the morning, the sun whitens the glass
and the suited shadows step out on the street
to do business; he leaves his bed
and quietly crosses the room to the box,
then to the stove,
setting a pan of water over the blue flame.
Arrows of light enter, rumple the blankets,
ignite his fingers. He dips the cocoons

into the layers of steam and water,
until they float to the surface
and are skimmed off,
as one man would strop the foam from his beer
or another clears the skies
on an autumn day. The only hint of a storm:

a thimble of broken leaves,
the thread of dust
winding, like an invisible path, to the gates
where God is a yellow moth

that flutters the eyelids open
and the day begins again.

II

Like silk, I am spun on two families—
the tree and the cloud,
the branch respecting the sky that flees
from itself.

It was after the war and my father was home,
my uncles, cousins—all men
flew back to their families,
except for my grandfathers
who heard the rumbling from their graves.
Times were good and everyone had their silks:

my aunts, black market stockings
that they wore in the cities,
my father his flier's maps of Formosa
and the Philippines folded in the dresser,
and the ash trees their veils of rust-colored leaves.

In September, on the day of my birth,
the translucent fibers filled the air,
sticking to cars, windows, fences and tree trunks.

Blown over on his back, a caterpillar
begged the wind to help him look for his shoes.

III

I am now the person you know,
you can see who I am.

I step out of the bath and walk to the bedroom;
I will not change again without warning.

There,
on the bed, are my pajamas,
woven and stitched in Taiwan.
A lotus for each breast and one
for each crazy bone.

An old woman hung them over a branch
and lowered it into the blue river;
a man with one leg eased the elastic
into the waistband; a new housewife
fastened the frog at the neck
and kissed it when no one was looking,
then packed them into a box marked *America*.
I wear this history, this secondhand clothing,
and still I am the person you know.

I blot the moisture off my back,
unpin my hair, and put them on:

this is the ascot, the tiny glove, the chemise;
this is the sleeping gown of the worm.
How lucky I am!
What dreams I will have.

But I will not change again without warning.

IV *Ailanthus*

It has learned the contours of America well:
the arc of its branches, the fatness of stones
and flexibility of leaves
where it curls.
It has a sixth sense for progress
and readies itself for a new contribution.

Ailanthus stops eating,
throws up what's left of its name
from the infinite caves of intestines,
and chooses its twig
as a woman would pick a man
for his stability and uprightness.
It returns its earthly possessions
to the *tree of heaven*,
and wades into the shallow pond
of its own mucus, quivering
like a wick, the flame
waxed over.

A true Christian,
this creature covers its head first
with a fine veil, leaving a space
through which it will see the sky again
one day, after the Cross has passed over
and the last shadow is gone from the earth.

We call this *a worm*
as it coils into the final,
veinous skin of its own life
and makes fools of us all.

v

Eggshell, sperm case,
bed sheet and burrow lining,
hinges, trapdoors,
noose or dragline,
the gossamer takes to air
at the whim of a current—
life is not easy.

Men with money on their minds
brought ailanthus to this country,
like rum or the blacks,
but my mother brought me.
Don't tell me how fortunate I am,
how rich. Like the others

I go out, set up my table at the corner,
and open my pockets
before the sun has left the market.
I flatter,
contrive purposes, imagine colors
no one would wear,
and hawk these goods.

Calling, *the essence of snow,*
cloud morsel, a skin
so much finer than your own,
I speak magic, but breathe the dust.

It clouds the air
as I tip the box over, tapping
the last fragments, the wings and scales,
wiping the wood for a new day.

Ailanthus, no one said
the branch leading to heaven
would be beautiful.
We take our silks from its thorns
and musty odor,
from its molded leaves.

FROM *TAKING TO WATER* (1984)

DIVING FOR ATLANTIS

for Ada

In a flush of leafless gum and alder,
the old Fourth Street Y
where the run-off from swamps
and secret southern tides collects.
On cold afternoons,
the black kids come here to dive
for what one says is *Atlanta,*
an island floating miles beneath
the fractured basin of this pool,
loaded with all the precious stones
their mothers promised them
in lullabies. Like the gulls
or kingfishers cracking the slate swells
200 miles from here, down they go
shooting up again and again
through the wreath of bubbles
to the surface, screaming
found it, found it.

Who in this city
smelling of scorched tobacco
and hickory dust would believe
what they can't see or sell,
so much water slipping through fingers?
Like the old woman lounging
on a faded towel, winter settles
into an armchair padded with dead leaves
and counts its treasure—
all the white faces glistening like dimes,
all the blacks bearing out
the same cold. But here,

a child in a pair of scissored trousers
leaps into the water and learns
to hold his breath until
the vision comes and the sunlight
slices him into every color.

Lady, the woman tells me, *Methodists*
don't take to water,
but I'm learning.
It's the Baptists who walk into lakes
and leave the rest of us
standing on the shore.

And I believe that even hers,
the heaviest earthbound body,
can hold air and float
on those seven veils of blue.
When I plunge headfirst,
joining her and all the others,
my flesh steeps and the steam rises
off the surface. I believe
that those who swim in winter
shed ghosts like these
whose sweet alum tears fall
to something larger, a sea
that never freezes over,
whose gentle pulse carries them
away from the Y, from this city,
to the shores of Atlanta
where, when they surface,
they will send for us.

CATFISH

By 6 A.M., the catfish
freshened on ice
have lost their pallor
and look like something
you'd want to eat.
A line snakes through the shadows
down Trade Street
where the last person stoops
to read the paper he brought
to wrap his fish in.
It takes pliers to open
a catfish plugged with tin and algae.
But the small ones, delicate,
dipped in batter,
are like white roses
blooming on grease.

I don't know what the sun
will mean to this winter day,
already sinking into the brick
and steam. But those who've left
their beds, their children,
their frozen corners
to stand in line outside the market,
hope it will shine forever,
radiant as the gaze of one
who swims through both mud and ink.

My friend feeds more sticks
to the fire and the flames jump
to the stained kettle of greens.

She tells me a dream she had
of a vacant strand on the Outer Banks,
and a flounder she found
with both faces up to the sun.
When she flicked it over
with another stick,
she saw her eyes, her own
slow smile, even her soul scattered
by gulls on the ribbons of sand.

Now she can't eat fish—
even catfish
which will eat anything.

In the dawn, mine is the only face
that loses its darkness.
I place my change on the glass
and reach into the strange aquarium
where the fish are stacked
in even numbers. Their fins
and whiskers are touching
as though they still know
who loves and hates them.

In the South,
fish are cooked in lard,
lard in greens, and greens
in warm silty water.
And when rings rise
to the unbroken surface,

then you know it is true.
The stars move to another pond
and a mewing starts up
in the trees.

TWO TREES

This summer they are saying
that two trees which never did before
swayed toward each other,
mingling leaves.
Shedding their powders at the same time,
they made a pact with the wind.
And from the kitchen table,
I can see the shadows shift
as the pecan breathes in the sunlight.
I wonder if this giant,
the grandfather of our back field,
still has what it takes
under those tendons of bark,
the layers riddled by seasons of birds,
or if the young dogwood tipped with green
will surprise us next March.

There's a deaf kid down the street
who can imitate the passion-
sounds of trees, the groan
and creak of branches so well
that he frightens the old Southern ladies.
Like the wind, he runs a clean path
up their driveways, or drops his bike
and watches for hours as I tear
the weeds, the heart-shaped leaves
of creeper from the gray coiled trunks.
Sometimes, he is so quiet and serious
that I stop what I'm doing
and take a second look.

It is true that we hear
what we want. Yet, these tears
are not for the silence between us
or the shriek of limbs suddenly bared
to the day's dazzling light.
They are the loving itch
of bud and dust, germ and sugar,
the little urges of oak and ash.
Like the vines, I accept their invitations.
I let my own green rags fall
to the ground, believing the sky
will meet all our demands.

Your first song to the stream of light
you drink with milk each morning.
A mockingbird spins its litter
of feathers and steals the rest.
Suddenly, he appears before you
in your highchair: spectacles,
a woolen shirt too warm for May.
His breath smelling of wine
and varnish, he croons back,
oy, oy, my little one,
like the faithful chorus
over his grave forty years ago.

He stoops to study your face
and I try to explain that
he is your great-great-grandfather
on your father's side,
a carver of bars
who left his wife and children
to make roses in America.
He blows the dust of birch and cherry,
of Russian forests from his nails,
and smoothes your cheek, *eat more...*
More! As though pleading could fatten
those palms and knees rubbed raw
from chasing wings of dust
across the floor.

It is rare, I think, such tenderness
and nerve in a man—
enough to make a woman follow him
from one land to another.
Eggs, a little herring, tea.
I give him these
and ask what door in this house
I've left open for him,
and how he came to find our street
from that steamy Concourse in the Bronx,
that loop of virgin trees
outside of Czernowitz.

But he answers in another language,
blessing the trees and this child
who sings into his ghostly ears.
We hear the angel close the door
a second time. How quickly,
the sun takes his place,
the mockingbird sings
as she shreds a crown of phlox
and silences her young.

THE MORAVIAN CEMETERY: "GOD'S ACRE"

I kneel down, rub the veil
of rain like a balm
into the cold black stone
and read the name, *Anne,*
the mother of three sons,
carved out by a man
who never touched her cheek
or lips, or asked
how life goes on.

But it never ends for those
who always knew where
they were going. For *Jacob,*
tobacco merchant,
the slab of fescue rolls out,
a plot in the next world.
I think a pious man
would have looked down
this long row of stones,
into the valley of cedars
and elms, and seen himself
and kept silent.

Yet, these plain marble faces
make me nervous. Scrubbed clean
each spring, they shone
in rain a hundred years
before the Greeks, the Blacks,
and Baptists entered this graveyard
with their scrolls and trumpet flowers.

The truth does not rest.
It paces the ragged path
past the mounds behind me,
waiting for one man
who refused to die,
who simply *fell asleep*
in 1871.

The shudder of sparrows
will not wake him,
nor the wind that lifts
a stash of seeds from the grass
and carries them off.
There are some secrets
the sky keeps to itself.

CHARTRES

I

Tuesday, the most human of days,
and the rain and wind
have left a path of broken geraniums
to the church. Inside, two nuns
from a Breton abbey pass in silence.
The hard white wings of their bonnets
brush against each other.
The air figure-eights
across the vaulted ceiling, wedding
stones so dark I can't see their faces.
Yet, I believe how tall that darkness is,
its huge blue eyes teared
by rain and the labor of hands
that laid each pane in place
at such great heights.

2

As a child, I could never pray
in front of others.
But there were shapes in the night
I could run my hand the length of
until I entered those glowing scenes
inside myself. This evening,
in another room, the moon hangs
prisms in the chestnuts.
The sky is sleeping,
wrapped in its pelt of stars,
and you and I in the darkness so tall

it must stoop to offer its love.
Soon, we will leave as we came,
for the arc of our bodies
over quiet space is the first window.

MAP FOR THE UNBORN

1

He pulled me up from the bed of goldenrod
and with a few quick strokes
brushed the grass, the yellow sparks
from my hair and shoulders.
The road entered the mountains
like a twisted key, letting light
into the darkened valley of cedar and oak.
When we asked *how far to Vernazza*,
the old man's fingers arched over the sea.
Another going the opposite way
simply shrugged and slapped the insects
off his thighs. Finally, a family,
mostly mothers and daughters,
gave many directions. The wind was confused
for these hills had many paths
and the sea spun a thousand threads
in one day. A woman could wear
the same dress her whole life
and still bear a dozen
who would vanish everywhere.

2

After nine months,
you will avoid the heat of the road,
the carelessness of strangers
to travel by water.
There is a small boat rocking
in the cove. Soon, you will slip
the dark rope from its mooring

and row as far as anyone can,
through the curve of fin and bone.

They say no one turns back
on this voyage, though a few swallow
too much sky or water,
and others cry out for nights after.
But then, who remembers these things?

Who remembers the blade of stars
pointing the way,
stars that will fall on the blackened tides
and shine even there, like the eyes
of those who are coming to us?

    3

We can only dream of the fingers
of land tying the seas together,
and these dreams are our only maps.

Follow the line that runs
from the thumb to the heart
until lines cover your face
and your legs give in.
Circle the mound of your smallest finger
twice around the world
until your fortune comes and goes
and a villager opens his window
to call you inside.

He will take your hand

and ask to hear your stories,
for you have crossed the seas
of your mother, and who can remember
having traveled so far?

CINQUE TERRE:
THE LAND OF FIVE NOISES

for Shula

In the summer, the Monterossans are even noisier:
the Communists and Socialists, sponge dealers
and women returning home at dark.
Children shout the fish from the shallows,
the rats back into the rocky shadows of the sea wall.
Only lovers get by in silence.

Even in that moment between words
when breath goes up in light
and utterance is impossible,
a motorbike stutters through the village
and two more after it,
or a train thrashes through a mossy gorge
toward the sea. Dreams are unnecessary—
talked away, like the bruised seawater
pulling out of the enormous caves.
Only sleeping stops the rumors
when a trace of color,
like the stain of peppers on muslin,
rushes the motionless faces.

Yet, a few things can be explained
by all this racket. Life must be named,
called back often before it wanders too far.
And so, a mother lifts her skirt
and slowly wades into the water
after a child who would rather follow
the fish to their smoky depths.

Also, there are always those
who mean nothing when they speak,
who, like birds, love the sound of air so much
they wave their arms, their tongues
and give it away.

THE OLD CITY

After the sun goes down,
you can hear the insects in the walls
of this old hotel—300-year-old ants,
roaches still wearing the royal colors,
demanding the dust be swept from their villas,
issuing orders someone must carry out.

Downstairs,
the young dishwasher steps out of the steam,
the streak of silver and china,
to take a break in the alley.
He shares his cigarette with the night.
The women sitting by their windows
peer into the darkness,
their arms folded on the sills
like soft ocher stones.

They study the night
to see how far they have to go
before their work is done.

The street winds forever
through rooms that are coming from dust
and going back to it.
The shadows are huge and endless
as the song of a young man
whose voice can't crack the walls,
send anyone into hiding,
or bring silence,
for this world is never finished.

THE BRIDGE
OF SAINT-BÉNÉZET

Sur le pont d'Avignon
on y danse, on y danse…

I pinch the flame
and the milky stump drowns slowly
into itself. Often,
the night joins us before the streets
of Avignon are quiet
and the day's newspaper has blown
into the river, blurring
under the wash of stars.

Above the Rhône,
the popes sold their blessings
and the sun went down every night
for a hundred and thirty years
as though light were gold
and the frail reeds could bear
its weight. The bastard children
left their mothers' houses
and climbed the path in darkness
to the palace where he waited.
For each, a sermon,
the nudge of a grizzled cheek
turned on a satin pillow.
But, at dawn, only Bénézet,
the little one with no real father
or mother, saw the angel of stone
crossing the river and heard it
calling his name.

The bridge where the children danced
has crumbled into the water,
the wreath of voices whisked downstream.
The new day's sun presses the night
back into its wicks, the charred trunks
wading in slowly. And the children
who once edged their way past the hawkers
and carts laden with onions
are now this green finger
that touches the sea.

I think they must have hidden
down those endless cobbled streets,
their shoes and baskets emptied
of light as each wooden door
slammed shut for the last time.
Or wandered off into the groves
east of here after pears or small birds
that let themselves be caught.
And yet, on nights when the wind
flushes the swallows down in the grass,
the current changes.
You can see the delicate claw of a branch
almost wave as it floats by,
or a face from long ago
rise in an eddy. The silt swirls
over your boots as you kneel,
leaning to pull them out.

And, like the stars, out they come.

FROM *THE PILGRIM AMONG US* (1991)

CHESTNUTS FOR VERDI

Loose, drifting in pools
of black water, the gravel slushes
as a pair of peahens crosses
the path, stabbing for seeds.
The one I gather from a tuft of grass
pushing up the stones
is too large for them: a chestnut,
hard and glazed,
like the belly of a mare
or the unbroken shore of a piano
where a singer leans, pressing out
the notes into the morning's stillness.

And he is there, arched
over the yellowed keys, his silhouette
as soft as the fingers cupped
around this fruit. The sunlight
slips between the salon drapes,
and a wagon filled with
oak, birch, and chestnut
enters the scrolled gate.
Each new stump waits
for the gray lip of soil
with a patience only trees have.
While the birds come and go,
like lovers frightened
by their own strange music.

The paths shoot off everywhere—
into the trees, the fields,
and one to the maestro's door where
a woman waits with her coin dish
to take us in. Into a web of rooms
unlit by the morning, into a silence
as false as the flowers
old women leave on his grave.

Yet the chestnuts bulging
out of her pockets are there
for anyone to see. Now they can
bring fire to a man's touch
and they'll do nicely in a pudding.
And the snow-tipped branches
which they left behind
rise and fall like heavy arms
coaxing the air, keeping
the music of the earth
close to the earth.

Roncole, 1984

IN JUST ONE DAY

The sun is waking in the high, stony cradle
of the Mottarone. It is gathered
into the sycamore's flailing arms,
the pine's sober gaze,
and dipped into black water
until it wails and the water fills
with light and the wailing
is the wind itself, the breath
of St. Julius pushing the small, white boats
across to the other side.

Smack! The woman laughs for God
and all the others as she slaps
the wake with her fat, brown palm,
pretending to kill the dragon and the snakes
that surface in our thoughts
as we near the island.
The boatman chuckles easily,
and her friends wish that they
had thought of flirting,
of kneading the sunlight and wind,
this burly man whose shirt flaps,
like a red flag, on his chest.

She laughs here, but she'll be the first
to kneel down on the cold slate steps
when we reach the shrine,
to kiss the pointed toes of the gold
threaded slippers, to run her fingers
the length of glass, the linen
nipped and tucked

where the curves of a body should be.
And the first to faint when
her eyes meet the empty sockets
of the skull, the grin
of St. Julius returning her passion.

Now that I've taken the water of this lake
into my own hands, I believe
almost anything. That the people
brought their fears here
and watched the last knot snakes
slip away from the mossy banks
to their sad slumber.
That they were chased by a madman
who was once just a man
in a soiled gown, tripping
through the trees and stones.
That the people paid him
with their hearts as the wind
lifted the leaves, spun them,
and let them settle again.
That this man,
who is now a saint, could come
down from his bed of silks,
from his sleep, come down
to this lady laid out cold in ecstasy
and silent for the first time;
that his bones could make
the twin dragons of her breasts
heave and struggle for air…

There are things I can't imagine.
Her friends pat her cheeks,
pull her up and make their way
back to the dock. In just one day,
the sun has left the Mottarone
and gone out into the world.
In just one day, it has grown old,
trying to sort the pilgrim
from the rest of us.

VALLEY SPORES

The best ones spring right up
from rain-soaked piles
of dung. My son laughs
as his grandfather tries to explain
how the bruised spring sky
enters an unwilling earth
and works its magic.

On Sunday evenings, I'd stand
at the sink, watching
my father and mother peel back
the pale hides, rinse,
and let them float, stem-up,
until they gleamed, like bowls
set out for creatures even
smaller than I. No chanterelle,
this plain valley spore.
Neither funnel, bell, nor star.
But still, their undersides,
sow-pink at first, would blacken
in the steamy fungal broth.
The silt drifted to the bottom
of our cups as we drank.
And then I kissed them both
and went to bed, half-believing
I might never wake.

The best ones, he goes on,
thrive in the places
you never find, untouched
by ribbons of alkali.

But, if you do, if you climb
the braid of wire at dawn
and leap into the field,
you can see them everywhere,
their bald heads bobbing
in clusters. In stubble,
mud, and witchgrass, hundreds
to fill a bathtub, or
to leave their smeared,
black moons beneath you. Everywhere,
when only seconds before
you looked and nothing bloomed.

SAC-RA-MEN-TO, CAL-I-FOR-NIA

          The vilest curse
a woman could utter in those days.
Not her husband nor the maid
nor the pigeons on the stoop,
swallowing their portion
of morning light could imagine
such a place. The precise syllables
of a sudden rage: *Sac-ra-men-to,*
whenever her fingers grazed
the rim of a hot skillet
or the iceman left his tracks
in the hall. *Sac-ra-men-to, Cal-i-for-nia,*
if snow came a day early and
without warning. Her accent blackened
the name of that place out west
as though life in this city
were the beginning and end of it.
But, even here in New York,
she had been left behind, this woman
who still double-knotted her apron and
kept fish for the evening's supper
in the bath downstairs. This woman
who powdered her arms with the flour
she had saved for the hens.
A mind both practical and eastern.
But why did her heart keep taking voyages?

          Outside, Vyse Avenue
and the first icy winds blow up
wads of news from the grocer's crates.
The new world, she thinks,

first it's seen and then eaten.
Farther down the street,
the sacred wall of the Bronx Zoo
with its huge baskets of parrots,
its sultry leopards, all the creatures
misplaced in this world. Perhaps
she would be the one to lead them
away from the ashen skies
of 1930. Over the stubble
of the plains, over those mythical peaks
to that shadowed city where, they say,
a woman can ripen at night
and flowers open all winter long.
Where dust settles around you,
shimmering, like an oath you take
only once in your life.

ELEGY ON VALENTINE'S DAY

Like a bundle wrapped
in white cloth, the first light
drops through the old boughs
of camphor. The children kneel
on the ground to open it
and roll it in their sweaters
with their sacks of food and fistfuls
of stones. When I was a child
and you'd ask how much
I loved you, I'd spread my hands,
a small queen setting
the boundaries of sunlight
on the known world.
But your arms were longer
and when it was your turn,
you would take me
a little farther each time.

On the flat edge of town,
the gift of light dissolves
between the rows where a farmer
has set his geese to weed.
And what they don't eat,
he'll cut and scatter, so that
by late afternoon
the whole gray field shimmers
down to the last feather,
the last furred root.

The light makes it clear
who is with us and who has gone.
In my palm, its lacy edges
fill with darkness, with a message
that touches the sky
and pulls the simplest life
from those branches: you are gone.
You have packed your bags
with neither day nor night
but with the dust of this valley
and left it. Then I remember
that when you were young,
this town and its fields were one
and the same and you could say
you came from both
without lying, without having
to hold a stone behind your back.

Now the farmer lifts his hat
to the last train, the caravan
of faces crossing his land
as night overtakes them.
And what did this day have to do
with love? You won't tell me.
And others forget or won't say.
Though the geese whine at its passing.
Though the sky pours itself out
on the cool grass below.

    for V. C. S.
    1896–1985

IN THE MOON

1

There are lots of men in the moon,
my son claims, and they all
have dirty feet. Sometimes they march
and the light swells.
Sometimes they lie down
and their mud-caked soles
nearly touch the earth like his
as he races toward the clear
winter sky where earlier
the moon rose between two palms.

2

On a night even colder than this,
she must have been listening
for those soiled boots
moving slowly in her direction.
Anna Akhmatova barely breathed each time
the wind slapped the shutters.
Resting her arms on the crude
wooden table, she pulled
each piece of shell
from the egg she held in her fingers.
"It's like peeling the moon,"
she said. She had brought
this, the first egg of their winter,
to the house of her friends
who watched in silence
as she sliced into thirds
the white, the yolk bruised,

like a sun gone out,
then pushed the plate
in their direction.

    3

A single egg all winter—
life being what it was
fifty years before my son's birth.
We must still learn to share
what was never ours.
Whether that rubbery light
which bends to our fancy
or the third translucent slice
of cucumber he sneaks
from the salad. Or the smaller
half-moons of his nails
as he yawns and slips his hand
into mine and we finally
walk side by side,
the dark ring of his lips
making a night all its own.

    4

The moonlight is as helpless
as those who tried to gather it
for warmth, like something
you could live by if you had to.
And when those men came down
from there and kicked in
the door to that small room

where the three sat,
kicked over the table and chairs,
the bits of shell scattered,
like a dream, and could
never be found again.

5

In his dreams, he calls out
though he does not wake
or know me. I think
of the crows he heckled today,
the black knives of their wings
cutting the air above us.
Of children's fists thrown up
in play, like stones
at the promise of heaven.
And of that leaf pile
left to darken and crumble,
suddenly let loose so that
the leaves cross the light and,
in falling back to earth,
step toward him.
I think of my own fears
and my love which is greater,
and how I will tell them,
as I tell the others
they must take off their shoes
before they enter.

DANCE

Two trumpets from the Mexican radio station
weave their scales through the dry leaves,
the still morning air.
Across the alley, our neighbor sways
as he hoses off a car so dark,
so weighted down with chrome and leather
that it is sinking inch by inch
into the muddy pool of his yard.
Suddenly, it is easier for me
to stand with my bundle of weeds,
to rise gracefully above the rose and zinnia
broken by a summer wind.
To the waves of music, I would like
to take another by the hand
and go out on a sunlit dance floor,
like a woman I saw once
in a satin skirt whose plump, brown knees
set the direction both she
and her partner would travel.
What keeps one man at a distance
can bring another closer.
Beneath this armful of shattered leaves
and stems that will not budge,
my body shines with sweat. And,
over the fence, I can see
the metal winking back
as he rubs it down with a soft cloth,
a vessel sturdier than these
I'm holding. A safe place
where two could meet in the dark
and find a rhythm to make the stars
and all the life beneath them whisper.

SOME VOICES

In the last days of October,
when clouds made the shapes of the dead,
we stretched our small bodies out
on the levee and sucked the crimson
out of pomegranate flesh.
Flat on our bellies and trying
to make the willows kiss
the gray water, we watched
their feathery shoots scrawl
on the surface the history of
a leaf flipped over or a stone
punted around the world
and back to this very spot.
A history of anything blessed
both with silence and the power
to break the sluggish surface
into light. Soon, something else
caught my eye: across the river,
the glint of a steel track
tracing the curves of an orchard.
And, peering out at that hour
from the streamer of windows,
faces that made us stand and watch
as though the slope of a cheek
or a waving hand could
bring life to the flatness
of this sky, this land.

*

I always knew where I came from,
but I couldn't believe it.

In childhood dreams, strong tides
carried off the mockingbirds
and the tufts of cotton
exploded in the night,
like Italian stars. At the station
a mile into town, my mother
straightened her stockings
and strangers thrummed on valises
and old uncles bowed, begging
for hugs. The crowd gathered
slowly, all smiles and tears,
until a man in a black cap,
his teeth like a keyboard,
sang out *Leaving for Corcoran.*
And nothing but steam filled the air.

*

Poor Corcoran.
Poor Shafter. Poor Taft.
The blunt steel nose pushes
its way through those
brief exhalations of dust.

Ain't no place to get off,
the man slumped beside me mumbles,
but I'm going there anyway.
A tumbleweed races us through town
and the ricks of cotton
stretch out like bones
along the rails. And he recalls
with a sudden sweetness

old lady Roosevelt back in the '30s
standing on those crates
in a sun hat wide as an ocean liner,
soothing the Okies with words
that swept the dust
right off their bread.

The women still come here, he says—
aunties, daughters, and the rest
to see their folks
at the new prison. Men who'll
leave *after a spell*, remembering
little but the heat and fog,
the sound of wheels grinding
in the middle of nowhere
like a woman's voice
as you fall off to sleep.

*

My son kneels down and places
a penny flat on the rail,
then sifts some gravel
into a pyramid. Seconds later,
he adds the torn sleeve of a foxtail
which has blown his way. Anything
that will let him touch
that huge, steamy body which
he has come to believe
is God. The yellow warning line
still two feet behind him,
he turns his head and rests

his ear on the track,
listening for the distant hum.
But when it comes, he reaches
for my hand and stays close.
The engine grows immense,
hissing; the glint of steel
blinds us. And as we start to
mount the silver steps, I can see
that he has already learned
some voices will take you anywhere.

THE NEST

The mockingbird throws open
her wings, and storms off
into the night. Soon
stars fill her empty nest.
The others come to look:
one to snitch a tuft of milkweed,
another to inspect the ragged seams.
Lastly, some stranger
in a black shirt, red cravat,
a mobster by daylight,
claims this hideout for himself
and his honey, the phoebe,
for the sweetness of night
has stunned them both.

Is it possible, all that
spit and polish come to nothing?
Or to those who never knew us,
never felt the ache of mud
and grass, these walls
through which we too will enter,
brushing the last fingers of air?
Already, my daughter
blows bubbles at me, flushes
and stares off at the light
spilling over the edges.

When she leaves, I'll lift
the windows and let them in—
the sparrow will rest on my pillow,
the wind fill my favorite dress.

Even the mockingbird will
pluck the mold and dust
from her feathers, and study
the mirror where I lift my child
to meet herself, and we laugh
at that other nest, shining,
filled with its endless rooms.

NIGHT SONG

Each evening, a new rhythm comes
when my foot pumps the rocker
worn down to bare wood.
We sway and doze though the sun
is still licking the sill.
Your eyes flutter open and close
each time the jays screech or
the children in the alley yell.
Why sleep at all, you
so full of this new life? Soon
you'll see how the night gathers up
all those glistening shards,
how it swallows the bickering
of the smallest creature.

Once, long ago, I learned how to
weave the last threads of light
into a ladder for anyone to climb.
For the man I imagined
resting on the roof of our house.
From up there, he could see
the colors rise with the dust
of this valley, and enter
the charred veins of its trees.
My mother didn't believe me.
No one was up there, she said,
or ever would be. But she was wrong.
I had heard the shadows sighing
as the beard of moonlight
swept the ground.

Not a sound now. My children
empty their hands in dreams.
Now I could fly out the window
and join the sparrows
huddled in the trees before dawn.
Or fold a moth back into the darkness
with the pages of this book.
Or I could hold myself
as gently as I've learned
to hold others. And who
would know? Listen:
the creaking branches, the shingles—
the small lights stepping
above us. Listen and sleep.

DUST

I

To survive this season,
you must get used to
the weeping, the crusted ear,
the thickening of the tongue
and brain. My son and I
brave an April wind
filled with its gray ghosts
for a trek to Blanco's bakery
to pick out his birthday cake.
For him, survival is a matter of
blending the grit of dust
with the buttercream stumps
of dinosaurs. He staggers
on the walk beside me, keeping
pace with the wind as it
dances over my shoes
and rises to a full waltz,
wrapping its flighty arms
around me. The pine trees
blanch and shimmer,
the lilies sag on their
last breath. And a pale mask
hides the cheeks of this boy
who blustered into life
six years ago and, like dust,
refused to settle.

2

Just weeks ago, we stood
by my grandmother's grave and
the wind stopped suddenly
as though she wanted to say
one place isn't another,
or to study the dress I had worn
for my visit. Then, the sun
broke through on every blade
and etching, every name
the dust had left behind.
Loam, sand, hardpan, rock—
layer upon layer, until the one
she might have been
and all my names for her
were lost. I laid the flowers down
and called for my child
lounging on a worn stone
to catch the light, the wind.
To feel for a moment
the old warmth of her fingers
stroking his cheek again.

3

A man might imagine an angel
of dust when, with my rags and bristles,
I turn glass back into air,
cheeks into roses.

The first rain and I lock arms, rejoicing.
But if I am *the angel of dust,*
unnamed by the gods
who huddled together, hiding
their eyes in their shawls
through this miserable season,
then what are the sparrows
wheezing in the locust trees?
And the grasshopper who lurches
into the rot of life?
And what are all the stars
reeling in their gritty capes?

4

At the back of the bakery,
in a darkened closet,
an old wooden barrel filled
with granules infinite and white,
as though the cosmos had disrobed
in private for the baker.
He closes the door behind him,
rubs his hands, and smiles
as he moves toward the counter
where we stand. In the light
of day are the dozens
which have risen for him
and will go out into the world
on the sweetened lips of the multitudes.

Row upon row on wire racks—
every color of confection,
powdered and cut, the sudden
rainbows of Creation.
Dust to dust? And I wonder
how we'll survive. Outside,
the sky moves too quickly
and the faces darken
long before night. *Don't worry,*
says Blanco, *a little light,*
a little sugar,
and we take the first bite.

ABOUT THE AUTHOR

ROBERTA SPEAR (1949–2003)

Roberta Spear's books are: *Silks* (1980), Holt, Rinehart and Winston, published as part of the National Poetry Series; *Taking to Water* (1984), Holt, Rinehart and Winston, winner of the 1985 PEN, Los Angeles Center, Poetry Award; and *The Pilgrim Among Us* (1991), Wesleyan University Press. She also won the James D. Phelan Award and was the recipient of writing grants from the NEA, the NEH, the John Simon Guggenheim Foundation, and the Ingram Merrill Foundation. Her poems have appeared in *Poetry Magazine,* for which she won the magazine's Frederick Bock Prize, and in *The New Yorker, The Atlantic Monthly, Crazy Horse, The Iowa Review, American Poetry Review,* and in several anthologies including *How Much Earth: The Fresno Poets.*

GREAT VALLEY

GREAT VALLEY BOOKS is an imprint of Heyday Books, Berkeley, California. Created in 2002 with a grant from The James Irvine Foundation and with the support of the Great Valley Center (Modesto, California), it strives to promote the rich literary, artistic, and cultural resources of California's Central Valley by publishing books of the highest merit and broadest interest. A selection of titles published by Great Valley Books includes:

Blithe Tomato, by Mike Madison

Bloodvine, by Aris Janigian

Dream Songs and Ceremony: Reflections on Traditional California Indian Dance, by Frank LaPena

Haslam's Valley, by Gerald Haslam

Highway 99: A Literary Journey through California's Great Central Valley, edited by Stan Yogi, Gayle Mak, and Patricia Wakida

Indian Summer: Traditional Life among the Choinumne Indians, by Thomas Jefferson Mayfield

Letters to the Valley: A Harvest of Memories, by David Mas Masumoto

Lion Singer, by Sylvia Ross

Magpies and Mayflies: An Introduction to Plants and Animals of the Central Valley and the Sierra Foothills, by Derek Madden, Ken Charters, and Cathy Snyder

No Time to Nap, by Mike Madison

Our Valley, Our Choice: Building a Livable Future for the San Joaquin Valley, by the Great Valley Center

Peace Is a Four-Letter Word, by Janet Nichols Lynch

Picturing California's Other Landscape: The Great Central Valley, edited by Heath Schenker

Skin Tax, by Tim Z. Hernandez

Workin' Man Blues: Country Music in California, by Gerald Haslam, with Alexandra Haslam Russell and Richard Chon

HEYDAY INSTITUTE

Since its founding in 1974, Heyday Books has occupied a unique niche in the publishing world, specializing in books that foster an understanding of the history, literature, art, environment, social issues, and culture of California and the West. We are a 501(c)(3) nonprofit organization based in Berkeley, California, serving a wide range of people and audiences.

We are grateful for the generous funding we've received for our publications and programs during the past year from foundations and more than three hundred individual donors. Major supporters include:

Anonymous; Anthony Andreas, Jr.; Audubon; Barnes & Noble bookstores; BayTree Fund; S. D. Bechtel, Jr., Foundation; Butler Koshland Fund; California Council for the Humanities; Candelaria Fund; Columbia Foundation; Federated Indians of Graton Rancheria; Wallace Alexander Gerbode Foundation; Marion E. Greene; Walter & Elise Haas Fund; Hopland Band of Pomo Indians; James Irvine Foundation; LEF Foundation; Michael McCone; Middletown Rancheria Tribal Council; National Endowment for the Arts; Poets & Writers; Rim of the World Interpretive Association; River Rock Casino; Alan Rosenus; San Francisco Foundation; Sandy Cold Shapero; L. J. Skaggs and Mary C. Skaggs Foundation; Swinterton Family Fund; Victorian Alliance; Tom White; and the Harold & Alma White Memorial Fund.

For more information about Heyday Institute, our publications and programs, please visit our website at www.heydaybooks.com.